BY ALLAN MOREY

THE CHICAGO
BEARS
STORY

BELLWETHER MEDIA • MINNEAPOLIS, MN

TM

Are you ready to take it to the extreme? Torque books thrust you into the action-packed world of sports, vehicles, mystery, and adventure. These books may include dirt, smoke, fire, and chilling tales. **WARNING** : read at your own risk.

This edition first published in 2017 by Bellwether Media, Inc.

No part of this publication may be reproduced in whole or in part without written permission of the publisher. For information regarding permission, write to Bellwether Media, Inc., Attention: Permissions Department, 5357 Penn Avenue South, Minneapolis, MN 55419.

Library of Congress Cataloging-in-Publication Data

Names: Morey, Allan.
Title: The Chicago Bears Story / by Allan Morey.
Description: Minneapolis, MN : Bellwether Media, Inc., 2017. | Series:
  Torque: NFL Teams | Includes bibliographical references and index.
Identifiers: LCCN 2015036438 | ISBN 9781626173606 (hardcover : alk. paper)
Subjects: LCSH: Chicago Bears (Football team)–History–Juvenile literature.
Classification: LCC GV956.C5 M67 2017 | DDC 796.332/640977311–dc23
LC record available at http://lccn.loc.gov/2015036438

Printed in the United States of America, North Mankato, MN.

TABLE OF CONTENTS

It is the **playoffs** for the 2010 season. **Quarterback** Jay Cutler drops back to pass for the Chicago Bears. He chucks the ball downfield. **Tight end** Greg Olsen makes a running catch. He rumbles into the end zone. Touchdown!

Jay Cutler

Greg
Olsen

After the extra point,
the Bears lead the Seattle
Seahawks 7 to 0. The winner
will go to the National
Football **Conference** (NFC)
Championship game.

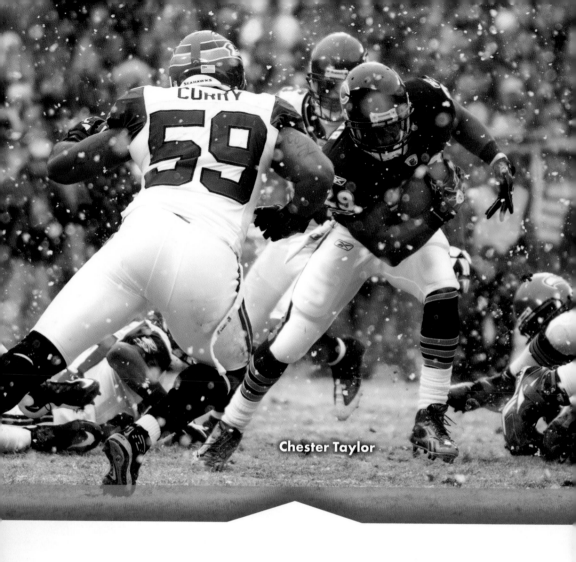

Chester Taylor

The Bears keep scoring. **Running back** Chester Taylor **rushes** for a touchdown. Cutler adds two more rushing touchdowns. The Bears are now up 28 to 0.

The Seahawks try to come back. They score several times. But it is not enough. The Bears win 35 to 24!

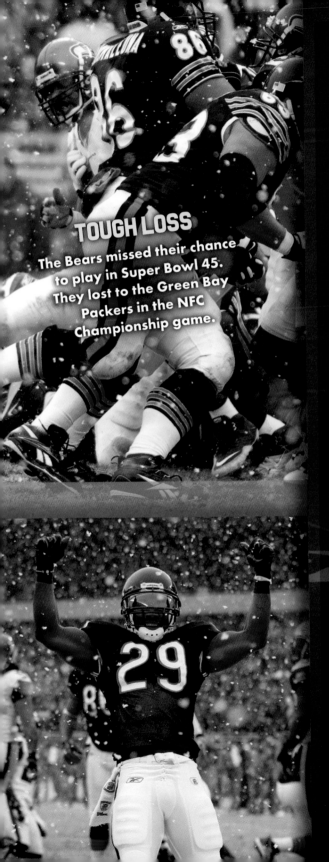

TOUGH LOSS

The Bears missed their chance to play in Super Bowl 45. They lost to the Green Bay Packers in the NFC Championship game.

SCORING TERMS

END ZONE

the area at each end of a football field; a team scores by entering the opponent's end zone with the football.

EXTRA POINT

a score that occurs when a kicker kicks the ball between the opponent's goal posts after a touchdown is scored; 1 point.

FIELD GOAL

a score that occurs when a kicker kicks the ball between the opponent's goal posts; 3 points.

SAFETY

a score that occurs when a player on offense is tackled behind his own goal line; 2 points for defense.

TOUCHDOWN

a score that occurs when a team crosses into its opponent's end zone with the football; 6 points.

TWO-POINT CONVERSION

a score that occurs when a team crosses into its opponent's end zone with the football after scoring a touchdown; 2 points.

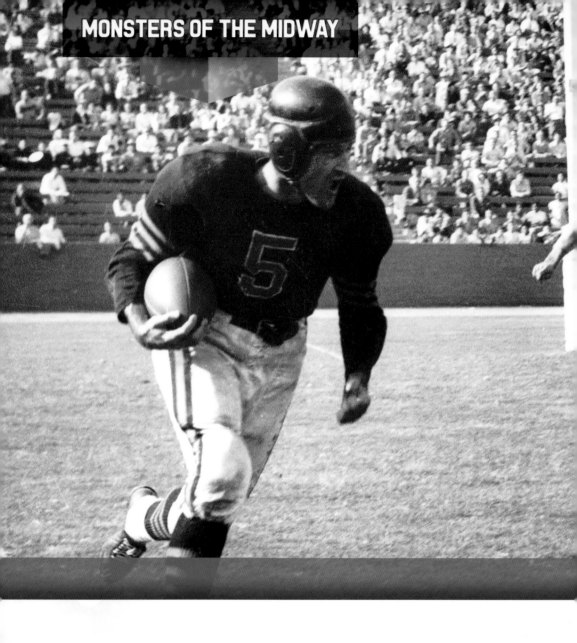

The Bears are one of the oldest teams in the National Football League (NFL). They have been around since its beginning. Back then, the team was called the Decatur Staleys.

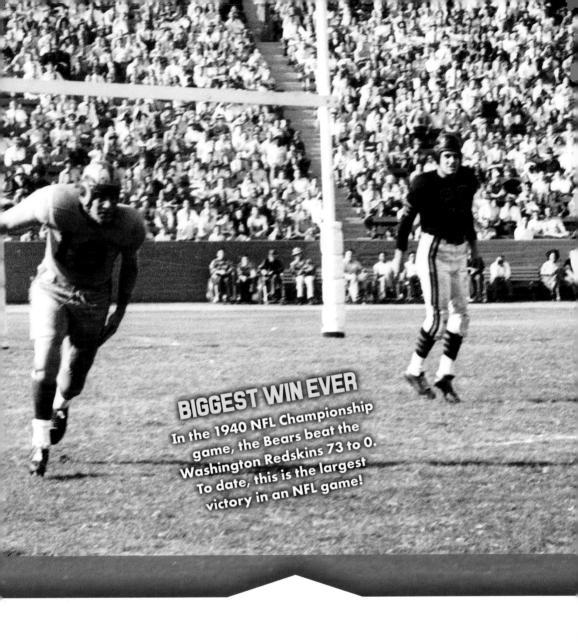

BIGGEST WIN EVER
In the 1940 NFL Championship game, the Bears beat the Washington Redskins 73 to 0. To date, this is the largest victory in an NFL game!

The Bears had some of their greatest successes in the 1940s. They won four league championships. Their strong **defense** earned them the nickname "Monsters of the Midway."

The Bears' first home was the small town of Decatur, Illinois. The team moved to Chicago in 1921. Playing in a big city meant more fans to support the team.

Since 1971, the Bears have played their home games at Soldier Field. This stadium is the oldest in the NFL. It first opened in 1924.

CHICAGO, ILLINOIS

PREVIOUS HOME
The Bears played at Wrigley Field from 1921 to 1970.

N
W E
S

The Chicago Bears joined the NFL in 1920. Back then, the league was organized differently than now.

Today, the Bears play in the NFC North **Division**. Their **rivals** include the Green Bay Packers, Minnesota Vikings, and Detroit Lions.

NFL DIVISIONS

 **AFC**

AFC **NORTH**

 BALTIMORE **RAVENS**

 CINCINNATI **BENGALS**

 CLEVELAND **BROWNS**

 PITTSBURGH **STEELERS**

AFC **EAST**

 BUFFALO **BILLS**

 MIAMI **DOLPHINS**

 NEW ENGLAND **PATRIOTS**

 NEW YORK **JETS**

AFC **SOUTH**

 HOUSTON **TEXANS**

 INDIANAPOLIS **COLTS**

 JACKSONVILLE **JAGUARS**

 TENNESSEE **TITANS**

AFC **WEST**

 DENVER **BRONCOS**

 KANSAS CITY **CHIEFS**

 OAKLAND **RAIDERS**

 SAN DIEGO **CHARGERS**

CUBS OR BEARS?

The Bears are named after Chicago's baseball team, the Cubs. This name fits because most football players are larger than baseball players.

NFC

NFC **NORTH**

CHICAGO
BEARS

DETROIT
LIONS

GREEN BAY
PACKERS

MINNESOTA
VIKINGS

NFC **EAST**

DALLAS
COWBOYS

NEW YORK
GIANTS

PHILADELPHIA
EAGLES

WASHINGTON
REDSKINS

NFC **SOUTH**

ATLANTA
FALCONS

CAROLINA
PANTHERS

NEW ORLEANS
SAINTS

TAMPA BAY
BUCCANEERS

NFC **WEST**

ARIZONA
CARDINALS

LOS ANGELES
RAMS

SAN FRANCISCO
49ERS

SEATTLE
SEAHAWKS

In 1919, businessman A.E. Staley wanted to start a **professional** football team. He hired George Halas to set it up. Together, they created a team with a bright future.

In 1921, Halas took control of the team. Under his leadership, the Bears won eight NFL Championships.

George Halas as player

George Halas as coach

PAPA BEAR

Halas played for, coached, and owned the Bears. He earned the name "Papa Bear."

George Halas as owner

After Halas, the Bears struggled. But the Monsters of the Midway were back in the 1980s. Led by a strong defense, they won **Super Bowl** 20.

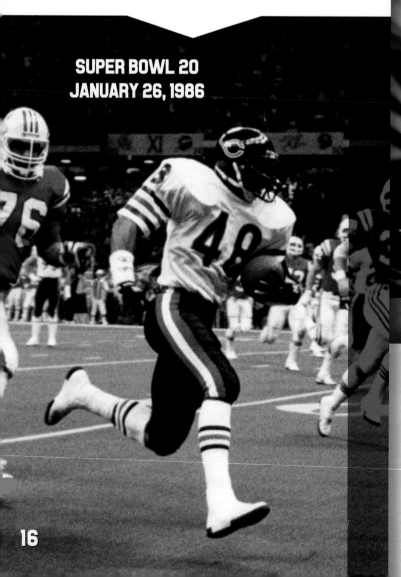

SUPER BOWL 20
JANUARY 26, 1986

Since their Super Bowl win, the Bears
have had some good seasons. They made
it to Super Bowl 41. But they lost to the
Indianapolis Colts.

TIMELINE

1920
Was a founding team of the NFL (as the Decatur Staleys)

1922
Changed name from Decatur Staleys to Chicago Bears

1940
Won their first of four NFL Championships between 1940 and 1946

1921
Moved to Chicago after George Halas took control

1921
Finished the season with the best NFL record

1933
Won first-ever NFL Championship game, beating the New York Giants (23–21)

1964

Drafted Hall-of-Fame linebacker Dick Butkus

1986

Won Super Bowl 20, beating the New England Patriots

46   FINAL SCORE   **10**

1975

Drafted Hall-of-Fame running back Walter Payton

2007

Played in Super Bowl 41, but lost to the Indianapolis Colts

17   FINAL SCORE   **29**

The Bears' **linebackers** have often been their star players. Dick Butkus was one of the best defensive players ever. He led the team in the 1960s and 1970s.

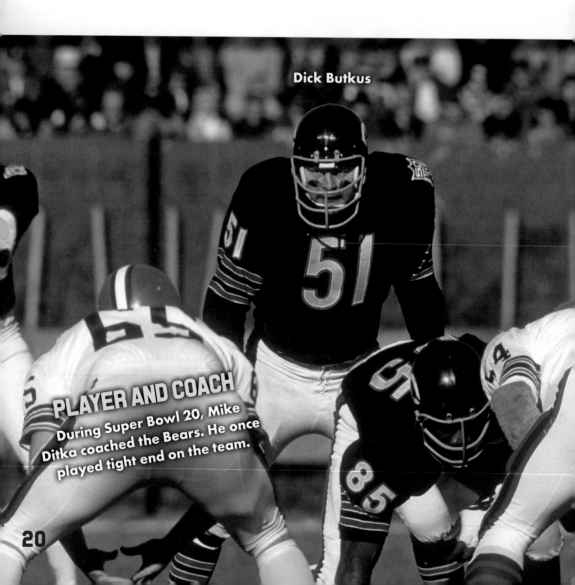

Dick Butkus

PLAYER AND COACH

During Super Bowl 20, Mike Ditka coached the Bears. He once played tight end on the team.

Brian Urlacher

In Super Bowl 20, the star on defense was Mike Singletary. During the 2000s, Brian Urlacher led the Bears' defense.

Speedy running backs have helped the Bears' **offense** score. Harold "Red" Grange was called "The Galloping Ghost." He was one of the NFL's first star players. All-time great Walter Payton ran for the Bears from 1975 to 1987.

Matt Forte rushed for touchdowns from 2008 to 2015. He was also a dangerous **receiver** out of the backfield.

TEAM GREATS

GEORGE HALAS (AS PLAYER)
DEFENSIVE END
1920-1929

HAROLD GRANGE
HALFBACK
1925, 1929-1934

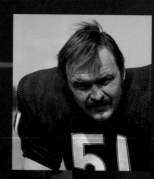

DICK BUTKUS
MIDDLE LINEBACKER
1965-1973

STAR STUDDED
The Bears have more members in the Pro Football Hall of Fame than any other team.

Matt Forte

WALTER PAYTON
RUNNING BACK
1975-1987

MIKE SINGLETARY
LINEBACKER
1981-1992

BRIAN URLACHER
LINEBACKER
2000-2012

Bears fans have seen many history-making games. One of the biggest was in 1932.

Back then, the team with the best record was crowned the winner of the season. But that year, the Bears and Portsmouth Spartans were tied. So they had a playoff game. Ever since, the NFL hosts a championship game.

EARLY CHAMPIONS
In 1932, the Bears beat the Portsmouth Spartans (now the Detroit Lions) 9 to 0.

Bears fans are loyal and **hardy**. Cold and windy weather does not stop fans from going early to home games.

THE SUPER BOWL SHUFFLE
For Super Bowl 20, the Bears recorded a song called "The Super Bowl Shuffle." They even made a music video for it!

They **tailgate** in the parking lot and share stories about their team.

MORE ABOUT THE
BEARS

Team name:
Chicago Bears

Team name explained:
**Named to go with the
city's baseball team,
the Cubs**

**Nicknames: Monsters of
the Midway, Da Bears**

Joined NFL: 1920

Conference: NFC

Division: North

**Main rivals: Green Bay Packers,
Minnesota Vikings**

Hometown:
Chicago, Illinois

Training camp location:
Olivet Nazarene University, Bourbonnais, Illinois

CHICAGO

N
W + E
S

ILLINOIS

Home stadium name: Soldier Field

Stadium opened: 1924 (Bears first played at Soldier Field in 1971)

Seats in stadium: 61,500

Logo: Wishbone C, which stands for Chicago

Colors: Blue and orange

SOLDIER FIELD

Mascot: Staley Da Bear

GLOSSARY

conference—a large grouping of sports teams that often play one another

defense—the group of players who try to stop the opposing team from scoring

division—a small grouping of sports teams that often play one another; usually there are several divisions of teams in a conference.

hardy—able to survive hard times

linebackers—players on defense whose main job is to make tackles and stop passes; linebackers stand just behind the defensive linemen.

offense—the group of players who try to move down the field and score

playoffs—the games played after the regular NFL season is over; playoff games determine which teams play in the Super Bowl.

professional—a player or team that makes money playing a sport

quarterback—a player on offense whose main job is to throw and hand off the ball

receiver—a player on offense whose main job is to catch passes from the quarterback

rivals—teams that are long-standing opponents

running back—a player on offense whose main job is to run with the ball

rushes—runs with the football

Super Bowl—the championship game for the NFL

tailgate—to have a cookout in the parking lot at a sporting event; a tailgate is also the door at the back of a pickup truck that flips down.

tight end—a player on offense whose main jobs are to catch the ball and block for teammates

TO LEARN MORE

AT THE LIBRARY

Burgess, Zack. *Meet the Chicago Bears.* Chicago, Ill.: Norwood House Press, 2016.

Howell, Brian. *Chicago Bears.* Mankato, Minn.: Child's World, 2015.

MacRae, Sloan. *The Chicago Bears.* New York, N.Y.: PowerKids Press, 2011.

ON THE WEB

Learning more about the Chicago Bears is as easy as 1, 2, 3.

1. Go to www.factsurfer.com.

2. Enter "Chicago Bears" into the search box.

3. Click the "Surf" button and you will see a list of related web sites.

With factsurfer.com, finding more information is just a click away.

INDEX

The images in this book are reproduced through the courtesy of: Corbis, front cover (large, small), pp. 10-11, 11 (bottom right), 12-13, 14 (left), 16, 22 (left, middle) 22-23, 23 (left, middle, right), 24-25, 28; Bryan Yablonsky/ SportsChrome/ Newscom, pp. 4-5, 6-7; Brian Kersey/ UPI/ Newscom, p. 5; Jeff Haynes/ Reuters/ Newscom, p. 7; Vic Stein/ Getty Images, pp. 8-9; Deposit Photos/ Glow Images, pp. 12-13 (logos), 18-19 (logos), 28-29 (logos); NFL Photos/ AP Images, p. 14 (right), 19 (top left); Focus On Sport/ Getty Images, pp. 15, 20-21; Jeff Haynes/ Getty Images, pp. 16-17; Tribune Content Agency/ Alamy, p. 18 (top); Underwood Archives/ Getty Images, p. 18 (bottom); Richard Mackson/ Getty Images, p. 19 (top right); Jerry Coli, pp. 19 (bottom), 21; AP Images, p. 22 (right); Pro Football Hall of Fame/ AP Images, p. 25; Fort Worth Star-Telegram/ Getty Images, p. 26; Brian Kersey/ UPI/ Newscom, pp. 26-27; Max Herman, p. 29 (stadium); Dilip Vishwanat/ Getty Images, p. 29 (mascot).